ART I: UNIT TEN
ART APPRECIATION

CONTENTS

Author:	**Kyle Bennett, A.S.**
	Diane Sheehan, B.S./M.A.
Editor:	Alan Christopherson, M.S.
	Annette M. Walker, B.S.
Illustrators:	Lauren Durain, A.S.T.
	Keith Piccolo, B.F.A.
	Alpha Omega Graphics

Alpha Omega Publications®

804 N. 2nd Ave. E., Rock Rapids, IA 51246-1759
© MM by Alpha Omega Publications, Inc.   All rights reserved.
LIFEPAC is a registered trademark of Alpha Omega Publications, Inc.

ART APPRECIATION

Why do people produce art? It doesn't specifically supply anyone's needs for food, shelter or (in any implicit way) propagate the human race. Yet, every civilization of recorded history has created works of art. Likely we do it because we *like* it. It gives us pleasure, we record important events and memories, and we reflect on the meaning of life. Regardless of the medium, enjoy it. Its world is diverse and its expressions are exciting.

In keeping with this Unit series, we will focus on the nonverbal visual arts (rather than film, dance or theatre). However, the study of *all* art forms is valuable, for it is a rich and rewarding experience.

OBJECTIVES

Read these objectives. The objectives tell you what you should be able to do when you have successfully completed this Unit.

When you have finished this Unit, you should be able to:

1. Describe the purpose of art.

2. List the elements of art and design.

3. Explain the history and drives resulting in several recent art movements.

4. Identify famous works.

5. Describe the five dominant visual arts.

In the space provided below, write what you think you will learn from this Unit, what you would like to learn, and why you are interested in this topic.

_____

_____

_____

_____

_____

_____

_____

_____

_____

_____

Note: All vocabulary words in this Unit appear in **boldface** the first time they are used. If you are unsure of the meaning when you are reading, study the definitions given.

I. THE PURPOSE OF ART

The science of **aesthetics**, or the study of beauty and art, began in ancient Greece as "the philosophy of art". Greece's great thinkers mulled over the purpose of art in society, deciphering if its purpose was primarily a moral catalyst or historical documentation. But back then, the discussion was informal and tagged on to other philosophical disciplines. This science was finally given its name and formal acceptance in the academic world in the late 1700s.

THE AESTHETIC EXPERIENCE

Art primarily achieves two goals. First, it gives the viewer pleasure. Second, it communicates truths, ideas or concepts about reality, typically inspiring a deeper understanding or insight into humanity and morality. The fusion of these two experiences in a work of art is known as the **aesthetic experience**.

Creating art requires both a mastery of **form** and **concept**. The artist's objective is to take concepts and present them in a well-formed creation which results in both pleasure and learning for the viewer. Put simply, art comes out of the synthesis of concept and form.

Concept. In days of old, art was typically built around beliefs based in religion, morality, heroism, military conquest, or the greatness of states or kings. In more modern times, the attention has focused itself increasingly upon personal world views and emotions. Either way, art is a record of the images, impressions and world views of the artist.

Much of the long-lasting value of art is found in its concept, for it can be used to express emotions, teach ourselves about, and make a record of, other times and cultures. For example, a great deal of the current knowledge of Ancient Egypt comes from hieroglyphic writing. Much of our understanding about the Christianity of the Middle Ages can be seen in the iconographic way biblical figures are portrayed, to be consumed by the commoners. The Bible was only for the clergy. Therefore, images were used for veneration.

Form. A work with little "to say" is still pleasurable simply because of the form that it is in. For example, some forms of modern dance, as well as works in the Minimal Art movement (studied later) have little obvious "message" behind them, but are rather a study of shape or movement itself. Even without explicit content, the work is pleasant, interesting and beautiful.

Form is the beauty of design and order, placing images in a manner that is easily recognizable and succeeds in clear communication. For example, this Unit is written in a format for clarity. If random patches of text were deleted, the font size changed every two lines and all of the artwork upside down, we would fail to clearly communicate the content of the book. Therefore, this text is bound to a certain form because it is a carrier of important content.

In the fine art world, the tools of form are line, shape, texture, color and value (the **elements of art**) as well as balance, proportion, rhythm, dominance and unity (**elements of design**). Remember that the concept will always define how these elements are used. The old adage of "form always follows function" is the rule. For example, if you want to communicate the concept of "fear" in a painting, it is unlikely that you want to paint a pleasant scene of warm color. Even in those previous examples (Minimal Art) where little concept is obvious, the form itself *is* the concept. For example, in an orange statue of a simple cube, the artist likely desired to communicate the concept of an orange cube!

▶ **Exercise 1.1**

1.1   Define aesthetics.

_____

1.2   Where did the "philosophy of art" get its start?

_____

1.3   What are art's two goals?

_____

1.4   What is the artist's objective?

_____

1.5   Art comes out of the synthesis of what two elements?

_____

1.6   Where is most of the enduring value of art?

_____

1.7   Define form.

_____

1.8   List the five elements of art.

_____

1.9   List the five elements of design.

_____

1.10   Is a study of shape or movement alone, art?

_____

CRITICISM

Deciphering whether a work of art is "good" or not (a.k.a. **criticism**) is not a simple task. It requires a certain amount of personal opinion, and a great deal of historical knowledge. However, at least three basic questions help to serve as a guide.

1. How good (well-thought, deep, etc.) is the concept?

2. How well (according to the elements of art and design i.e. form) is it executed? To put it another way, is the concept clear?

3. Do you like it?

If a work ranks high before all three of these questions, it is likely to be "good" even "great." But art evaluation doesn't end with simple questions. A work may be excellent, but historically insignificant or vice versa. Reevaluate works throughout your lifetime, for there is often more to a work than is apparent at a first glance.

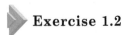

Exercise 1.2

1.11 Define criticism.

_____

1.12 What three questions serve as a guide when evaluating art?

a. _____

b. _____

c. _____

1.13 Are all excellent works of art regarded in history as such?

_____

. . . .

Review the material in this section in preparation for the Self Test. This Self Test will check your mastery of this particular section as well as your knowledge of the previous section.

SELF TEST 1

Answer these questions (each question 5 points).

1.01 Why do you enjoy art?

_____

1.02 For what three reasons do we create art?

a. _____

b. _____

c. _____

1.03 Define the aesthetic experience.

_____

1.04 Art comes out of the synthesis of what two elements?

_____

1.05 Whose images or world views does a work of art inevitably contain?

_____

1.06 Where does much of the enduring value of art come from?

_____

1.07 List the five elements of art.

_____

1.08 List the five elements of design.

_____

1.09 Define criticism.

_____

1.10. What three questions serve as a guide when evaluating art?

a. _____

b. _____

c. _____

40 / 50

Score _____

Instructor Check _____

Initial   Date

5

II. RECENT MOVEMENTS AND STYLES

The time periods covered in this section span from the middle of the eighteenth century to the present. For further reference and examples, a good historical art anthology may be necessary, for it is important to understand the historical context for each artist and their work. The student is encouraged to do library research to gain exposure to the various periods of art and explore representative works of each period.

18TH CENTURY

(Mid 1700s) Neoclassicism. The excavation of the ancient Greek and Roman cities of Pompeii and Herculaneum revealed the high cultural sophistication of these ancient peoples. Artists began to imitate their works. This primarily French movement produced beautifully crafted works stressing moralizing historical themes. (*The works of Jean Auguste Dominque Ingres and Jacques Louis David are good examples of Neoclassicism.*)

(1750–1850) Romanticism. A reaction against the "stiffness" of neoclassicism, it emphasized passion and intuition, not restraint or order. This resulted in works of bold light, deep shadow, containing exotic scenes of non western cultures, or self portraits. This movement also popularized the painting of landscapes, which hitherto had been shunned. (*Research the works of Eugene Delacroix and Jean-Honore Fragonard to experience further examples of Romanticism.*)

Giant Photos, Rockford, IL

JEAN–HONORE FRAGONARD'S
A YOUNG GIRL READING

19TH CENTURY

(Mid 1800s) Realism. A reaction against the idealism of both neoclassicism and romanticism, realism focused on objective, unsentimental, accurate (often dreary) depictions of common life, especially the work of peasants. Abandoning heroism, it often cynically commented (for the first time) on society and current events. These artists were aided by the benefits of new chemical pigments and photography. (*The works of Gustave Courbert and Jean Francois are good examples of further study into Realism.*)

Giant Photos, Rockford, IL.

JEAN FRANCOIS' THE GLEANERS

(1870–early 1900s) Impressionism. Impressionism was developed from the concept of present, immediate impressions of objects and events, focusing not on detail but impact. With a quickly done, sketchy feeling, impressionist works were often brilliant, informal outdoor scenes. (*Works by Pierre August Renoir (1814–1919) and Auguste Rodin are good examples of the Impressionistic style.*)

20ᵀᴴ CENTURY

Cubism. The most influential movement of modern art, Cubism was affected by African arts. In it, collected objects are reduced into geometric shapes and reassembled in order to shock and disturb. Planes, geometric forms, and angles play on a flat surface while multiple viewpoints dominate. (*Research Pablo Picasso. His works include many good examples of Cubism.*)

STARRY NIGHT, VINCENT VAN GOGH

THREE MUSICIANS, PABLO PICASSO (1921)

(Early 1900s) Expressionism. Artists sought to portray the emotions and responses that objects and events aroused in them. Expressionist artists sought to infuse nature with spiritual meaning, distorting it by personal interpretations of heroism or despair. It was similar to Romanticism in that it focused on personal vision, but differed in that beauty was primarily in the soul rather than nature itself. (*Research Van*

Gogh's (1853–1890) works to see a good cross-section of Expressionistic works.*)

(Italian, 1909–1916) Futurism. Futurists featured machines or figures in motion in attempt to portray the glorified power of the newly dawned machine age. It was undercut by an aesthetic desire to remove the old to make way for the new. (*Fernand Leger (1881–1955) is an artist that strongly represents Futurism in his works.*)

(1915-22) Dadaism. Meaning *nonsense* or *baby talk*, Dada was art containing no specific message, incorporating actual objects i.e. buttons, leaves, etc. into the work. Cubism was viewed as "too tame" in the post-WWI art world. Dada was a protest movement against what its purveyors saw as outworn artistic rules and traditions. (*The works of Marcel Duchamp (1887–1968) are good examples of Dada.*)

(1925) Surrealism. Developed from the psychological theories of Sigmund Freud, the main interest to the Surrealist was to paint the disturbing madness of a fantasy–like dream. They sought to liberate the creative mind from reason into the higher reality of hallucinations. Often painted oddly realistic to magnify the image's effect. (*The works of Salvador Dali (1904–1989) and Max Ernst represent the use of surrealism in their art.*)

©2000, Artists Rights Society (ARS), New York/ADAGP, Paris

MAX ERNST'S *EVERYONE HERE SPEAKS LATIN*

(1940s–1950s) Abstract Expressionism. The act of painting was more important than that which is painted. The product was not as important as the creative process itself. This resulted in simple splashes of paint presented

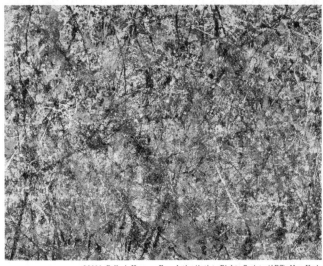

©2000, Pollock-Krasner Foundation/Artists Rights Society (ARS), New York

JACKSON POLLOCK'S *LAVENDER MIST*

as art. (*Research the works of Jackson Pollock (1912–1956) to experience more examples of Abstract Expressionism.*)

Pop Art used everyday images and common subjects, such as detergents, soup cans, boxes and other mass produced products. Often considered playful and not serious, its focus was to destroy what they viewed as the unnecessarily difficult parts of producing of fine art. Therefore, they utilized the simpler techniques of commercial art as they rejected the "superiority" of abstract art and reached out to the broader culture. (*Examine further the works of Roy Liechtenstein [comic strip themes] and Andy Warhol [soup cans, film icons] to demonstrate the validity of Pop Art.*)

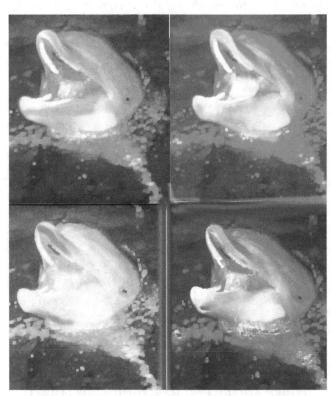

FLIPPER DIPTYCH—THIS IS AN EXAMPLE OF A WORK DONE IN THE SYLE OF ANDY WARHOL'S POP ART.

Optical (Op) Art. These works were intentional optical illusions that either altered depth perception (background is foreground, etc.), or seemed to flicker and pulsate. (*The works of Kenneth Noland [Chevron motifs, target series], and Ellsworth Kelly [background becomes the foreground] are excellent examples of Optical [Op] Art).*

Minimal Art. This movement typically consisted of abstract, three-dimensional geometric shapes of few colors. The focus was on line, shape and color itself without any deeper purpose. Primarily an American movement, artists included *Donald Judd* and *Lucas Samras*. Some in this movement would only design their work and have others construct it.

Kinetic Art. Kinetic art is work which includes physical movement, either physically or as a visual effect. *Alexander Calder's* mobiles are good examples of kinetic art.

Psychedelic Art. Dominant in the drug culture of the 1960s, and often used in concert posters of the era, this movement distorted visual perception by illustrating the exaggerated colors and movements often associated with hallucinogenic drugs.

Review the material in this section in preparation for the Self Test. This Self Test will check your mastery of this particular section as well as your knowledge of the previous section.

SELF TEST 2

Match the following terms with their descriptions (each answer 5 points).

2.01 _____ Expressionism

    a. imitation of Greek and Roman art, stressing moralizing historical themes

2.02 _____ Futurism

    b. focus on personal intuition, popularized landscapes

2.03 _____ Romanticism

    c. dreary depictions of the work of peasants

2.04 _____ Pop Art

    d. present, immediate impact of objects and events, sketchy outdoor scenes

2.05 _____ Kinetic Art

    e. planes and objects are reassembled in order to shock and disturb

2.06 _____ Psychedelic Art

    f. infused nature with spiritual meaning

2.07 _____ Neoclassicism

    g. glorified the new machine age

2.08 _____ Abstract Expressionism

    h. a step past Cubism, no specific message, incorporated actual objects

2.09 _____ Surrealism

    i. realistically painted, dreamlike visions, based on Freud

2.10 _____ Cubism

    j. act of painting more important than the product

2.11 _____ Minimal Art

    k. utilized commercial art techniques, reached out to a broader culture

2.12 _____ Realism

    l. optical illusions

2.13 _____ Op Art

    m. abstract three dimensional geometric shapes of little color or deeper meaning

2.14 _____ Dadaism

    n. art including physical movement

2.15 _____ Impressionism

    o. based on visions associated with hallucinogenic drugs

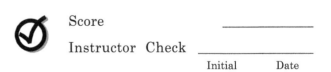

60	
	75

Score _____

Instructor Check _____

       Initial   Date

III. ART FORMS

The art forms of painting, sculpture, architecture and more recently commercial art, have all been influenced by the movements addressed in the previous chapter. Each plays a valuable part in our history, achievements and world views.

PAINTING

Perhaps the oldest recognized art form, it is certainly one of history's most important. Whether created for commission or personal pleasures, paintings are produced to communicate ideas in a visually exciting manner.

Portraits. The most popular subject in art history is man, for people themselves are painted more than anything else. This is likely because it helps the artist to connect with the viewers on their most basic levels. Portraits themselves evoke sympathy or even adoration, for human figures are often utilized as a symbol or concept rather than as a straight representation.

American Gothic was painted by previously unknown artist Grant Wood. In 1930 he submitted it to an annual exhibit of new art at the Art Institute of Chicago. It brought him overnight fame and lines of excited viewers. Though many farmers thought they were being ridiculed, Wood's intention was to display the hard working, dependability of Iowa farm people.

The *Mona Lisa* by Leonardo da Vinci (1452-1519) has been a mystery and fascination ever since he created it. The woman is smiling, but in what way? What is she looking at? What is Da Vinci saying?

The influential, fifty-year career of Spanish artist Pablo Picasso (1881-1973) encompassed

Art Institute of Chicago

GRANT WOOD'S *AMERICAN GOTHIC* (1930)

Louvre, Paris

LEONARDO DA VINCI'S *MONA LISA* (1503-05)

many divergent styles. He is most famous for pioneering the Cubist movement (see previous chapter). His *Weeping Woman* (1937) is an excellent example of that genre.

In it, a face is made from the shapes of broken glass and colors clash like flashing lights. What we see is not the portrait of a woman, but what happens to her face when she weeps: pain and tears. Picasso painted it in 1937 as a reaction to Spain's brutal Civil War.

WILLIAM HICKS' *THE PEACEABLE KINGDOM* (C.1840-1845)

A **Still Life** is a close up of objects often used to symbolize the bounty of nature or the wealth of patrons. Flowers and fruit are often immortalized, thus setting them against the decay that they inevitably endure. Some believe that a still-life gives the artist the greatest power to compose their work, since the artist has complete freedom to select and arrange the subjects.

At the worst moments of Dutch painter Vincent van Gogh's (1853-1890) life, he was insane, depressed and utterly lonely. However, in his *Fourteen Sunflowers in a Vase,* he manages to convey vitality and radiant splendor.

PABLO PICASSO'S *WEEPING WOMAN* **(1937)**

Animals. Animals are seen in paintings as old as cave art, and are often used in patterns or as symbols of meaning relating to human history, philosophy, etc.

Quaker minister and American folk painter Edward Hicks (1780-1847) painted *The Peaceable Kingdom* to reflect his non-violent philosophy. In it, "peace" is portrayed in two ways. In the foreground, animals that are natural enemies are lying together contentedly with unafraid children. In the background, Pennsylvania's founder William Penn is making peace with the Indians.

VAN GOGH'S *FOURTEEN SUNFLOWERS IN A VASE* **(1888)**

Landscapes and Seascapes emphasized the appearance, power and atmosphere of nature. A **landscape** is a picture representing a section of natural, inland scenery such as a prairie, woodland, mountains, etc. They have been used to stress the importance of owning land and seafaring. Chinese painted mountains on paper scrolls simply for the decorative, spiritual connotation they entailed. A **seascape** is a drawing, painting, etc. of a view of the sea, often containing a portion of the beach.

French artist Claude Monet (1840–1926) realized that colors within a scene change with the time of day. He carried several canvases, and as the light changed, he moved on to another painting. A lover of the sea, he painted many pictures of boating and swimming.

Philadelphia Museum of Art

CLAUDE MONET'S *POPLARS* (1891)

Murals. Cave art and Egyptian hieroglyphic writing are murals, but the great period of mural painting was during the Renaissance. Since 1900, there has been a revival of mural paintings on public buildings. It is used for either a decoration relating to the surrounding architecture or as social commentary.

One of the greatest in history, *The Last Supper,* was painted in the dining hall of a monastery. Painted on dry plaster, it shows the deep and complex emotions of each person at Christ's table, as well as Da Vinci's amazing knowledge of anatomy and perspective.

Santa Maria delle Grazie, Milan (©Planet Art—The Renaissance)

DA VINCI'S *THE LAST SUPPER* (1495-98)

Contemporary Mexican artist Diego Rivera (1886-1957) romanticizes the history, dignity, toil and sweat of Mexican peasants and laborers. His murals adorn the walls of public buildings throughout Mexico City. He also painted murals of American auto workers of the 1930s in Detroit, Michigan.

In *Detroit Industry, North Wall* (Detail), workers move in their space to the rhythm of their work. Auto workers move to a ballet of lines and shapes describing backbreaking work and human endurance.

Photo ©1991, Detroit Institute of Arts

DIEGO M. RIVERA, GIFT OF EDSEL B. FORD.

DETAIL—MURAL: *DETROIT INDUSTRY, NORTH WALL,* 1932-33

3.1   What is the most popular painted subject in history? Why?

_____

3.2   Who painted *American Gothic*? What was the response from farm workers?

_____

3.3   Where were animals first painted?

_____

3.4   Who painted *The Peaceable Kingdom*? What historical figure is represented?

_____

3.5   What are still lifes often used to symbolize?

_____

3.6   How does still life allow for the most creative composition?

_____

3.7   What have land and seascapes historically signified?

_____

3.8   Why did Claude Monet carry several canvasses?

_____

3.9   When was the great period of mural painting?

_____

3.10   What did Diego Rivera romanticize in his murals?

_____

ART

Ten

UNIT TEST

$\frac{80}{100}$

Name_____

Date _____

Score _____

ART APPRECIATION: UNIT TEN TEST

Answer these questions (each question 4 points).

1. Define criticism.

   _____

2. For what three reasons do we create art?

   a. _____

   b. _____

   c. _____

3. Define the aesthetic experience.

   _____

   _____

4. List the five elements of art.

   a. _____   c. _____   e. _____

   b. _____   d. _____

5. List the five elements of design.

   a. _____   c. _____   e. _____

   b. _____   d. _____

6. List the three basic questions that help serve as a guide when evaluating a work's value.

   a. _____

   b. _____

   c. _____

Matching (each answer 4 points).

7. _____ neoclassicism

8. _____ realism

9. _____ cubism

10. _____ surrealism

11. _____ abstract expressionism

12. _____ pop art

a. planes and objects are reassembled in order to shock and disturb

b. dreary depictions of the work of peasants

c. imitation of Greek and Roman art, stressing moralizing historical themes

d. utilized commercial art techniques, reached out to broader culture

e. act of painting more important than the finished product

f. realistically painted, dreamlike visions based on Freud

1

Answer these questions (each answer 4 points).

13.   What is the most popular painted subject in history? Why?

_____

_____

14.   Why did Claude Monet carry several canvasses?

_____

_____

15.   Define sculpture.

_____

16.   Define relief.

_____

17.   Why is architecture unique as a fine art?

_____

_____

Identify these house styles (each answer 4 points).

18.   _____

    a.   Classical Revival

    b.   Prairie

    c.   International

    d.   Organic

19.   _____

20.   _____

21.   _____

2

Answer these questions (each answer 4 points).

22. For what purpose were Greek temples built?

_____

_____

23. What was the intended result of Gothic architecture's inspirational atmosphere?

_____

_____

24. Define applied art.

_____

25. Why shouldn't the aesthetic value of commercial art be dismissed?

_____

_____

SCULPTURE

ALEXANDER G. EIFFEL'S *STATUE OF LIBERTY*

Sculpture is three dimensional art either carved out of (wood, ivory, stone) or molded from (clay, wax, glass) a substance. It has served as perhaps the greatest record of ancient history we have, for it breaks down much slower than other forms of art. It was used for m o n u m e n t s, memorials, personal expressions and decorative architectural features.

Most sculpture is **freestanding** (surrounded on all sides by space) and **In the Round** (all sides complete), such as the largest statue in the world, the Statue of Liberty.

Upland, California

AUGUST LEIMBACH'S *MADONNA OF THE TRAIL* **(1929)**

GUTZON BORGLUM'S *MOUNT RUSHMORE NATIONAL MEMORIAL*

Sculpture that is raised against a background is a **relief**, common in Egypt and on grave markers.

An **intaglio** is a reverse relief where the image is cut into a surface rather than raised from a background.

AN EGYPTIAN RELIEF

3.11   sculpture

_____

3.12   freestanding

_____

3.13   in the round

_____

3.14   relief

_____

3.15   intaglio

_____

ARCHITECTURE

The principles of art and design are just as necessary in architecture as in any other art form. But it is somewhat unique in that it must first be designed to fit a specific practical purpose (typically containing people), while remaining aesthetically pleasing. As in the first chapter addressing the science of aesthetics, form must follow function.

Architecture's form depends on its physical, historical and cultural environment, and as such it has evolved throughout history. In the past, it was common

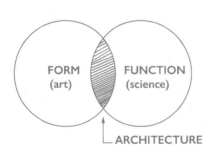

to find political messages as part of the structure itself, i.e. the majesty of God as contained in a church or a king in his palace. It also must be designed for the benefit of people's use. It must be able to stand up under its own weight, plus that of its contents; as it maintains a stable and comfortable environment. Also, materials and people must have convenient accessibility to entrances and exits.

Function. The architect must design a building that solidly meets its functional and aesthetic needs in the most cost-effective way possible, while building in durability.

The needs of the building may change. For example, a strip mall may someday be converted into a school. Therefore, the design must be flexible enough to not only meet the needs and desires of the commissioner(s), but also have other viable uses.

The environment must also be considered. For example, a group of Florida architects designed a shopping mall for a Utah city. They failed to consider the weight that snow would put on the roof. The result: the snow caused the roof to collapse. Therefore, the design must protect from extremes in weather, as well as the general concerns of resisting fire and earthquake.

As the concerns of beauty (aesthetics) and function conflict, the architect must create acceptable solutions.

Houses. Throughout history, home architecture has been bound by available materials, climate and lifestyles within cultures. The following are but a handful of popular styles.

Colonial

Colonial was one of the earliest
house styles in America.
It continues to be popular because
of its efficient use of materials
and its stately appearance.

strong, simple
gable with shed
towards front
and rear

small overhang,
or none at all

shutters

simple, unarticulated,
rectangular, two-story
mass

symmetrical facades

simple rectangular base
plan—may have additions
at rear

entry ornamentation

Classical Revival

The Classical Revival was a Renaissance
of Greek and Roman forms that swept America
in the mid-ninteenth century. Rich in symbol
and ornamentation, it was used on almost
every type of building which diluted its meaning.

grand scale–borrowed
from the Greek Temples

classical portico complete
with rich entablature, decorative
cornice and tri-parite columns.

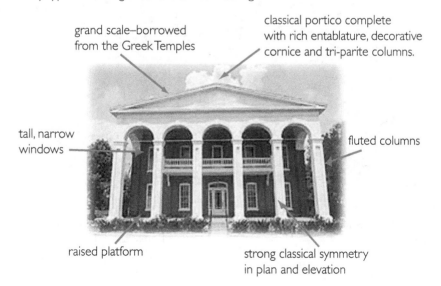

tall, narrow
windows

fluted columns

raised platform

strong classical symmetry
in plan and elevation

Prairie

Robie House, designed by Frank Lloyd Wright, 1902, Chicago, Illinois. 57th street elevation photo by Richard Nickel.

Prairie was the forerunner of
the Usonian House, predecessor to the
popular suburban "Ranch House".

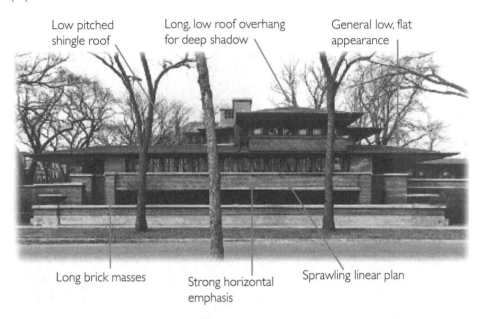

Low pitched
shingle roof

Long, low roof overhang
for deep shadow

General low, flat
appearance

Long brick masses

Strong horizontal
emphasis

Sprawling linear plan

Victorian

Victorian was born in the Victorian era.
It is a mixture of many styles,
but it especially borrows from Gothic Revival.
Technological advances of the age
such as the jigsaw are reflected in
the ornate wood detailing.

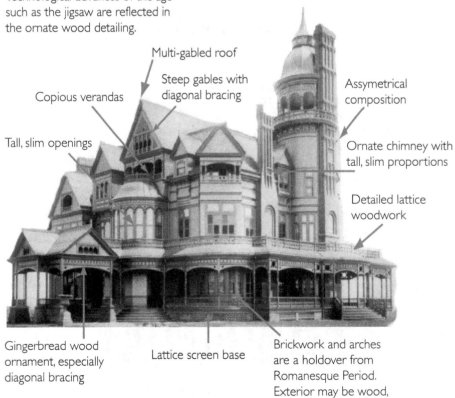

Multi-gabled roof

Steep gables with
diagonal bracing

Copious verandas

Assymetrical
composition

Tall, slim openings

Ornate chimney with
tall, slim proportions

Detailed lattice
woodwork

Gingerbread wood
ornament, especially
diagonal bracing

Lattice screen base

Brickwork and arches
are a holdover from
Romanesque Period.
Exterior may be wood,
but forms are similar.

18

Bungalow

Moonlight Bay Bed and Breakfast, Palacios, Texas, owned by Earl and Gaye Hudson.

Bungalow came
to the U.S. via the English
presence in India where the
Bengali house was a low structure
with porches all around.

Porch gable facing street

Many Gables in many directions

Capital Moldings

Column pedestals at porch

Slightly pointed arch at large porch span

Tapered wood columns

Slightly raised floor (wood framing on piers)

Large, covered porch- usually a partial wraparound

International

Villa Savoye, designed by Le Corbusier, Poisy, France, 1929.

International was not based implicitly
on cultural concerns, but was instead an attempt at using
modern structural materials to reinforce the personal
environmental concerns of light and air.
Non-essential ornamentation was abandoned in favor of purity of
form and abstract geometry. Functionality was the key to the style.

General horizontal expression employed using window strips and solid planes.

Flat roof

Geometric (square) Plan

Open, flexible interior around structural frame

Ribbon Windows

Exterior Wall expressed as a thin curtain

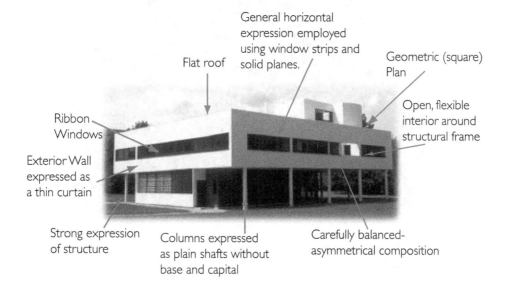

Strong expression of structure

Columns expressed as plain shafts without base and capital

Carefully balanced- asymmetrical composition

19

Organic

Still imaginary, this style comes from a desire to better fit the "natural world". Since it cannot be completely drawn, the owner must actively participate in the construction process.

Sculptural massing of curves without straight lines or right angles.

Irregular, free-form plan.

Shingles or sprayed gunite "skin" helps to keep it watertight.

Operable windows become difficult with this style.

Amalgamated

An attempt to combine too many materials and styles becomes awkward.

Temples and Churches. Because religion was central to the Greek culture, the temple was their single most important building. They did not gather inside their temple to worship. Rather, the temples were built as houses for their gods. Only priests and a few assistants were ever allowed inside. Everyone else prayed in front of the temple. For this reason, Greek temples did not have to take in the concerns of human habitation when planning the design.

They strove to make their temples perfectly proportioned, as seen in the famous Parthenon, which is encased in doric columns. Its sculptures are considered the greatest in the world. Originally a temple to a Greek goddess, the Parthenon was converted into a Christian church around A.D. 500. The layout was designed so that visitors would notice different

THE PARTHENON, GREECE

details as they drew closer. The columns are slanted towards the top. If the columns were extended for a mile, that is exactly where they would meet.

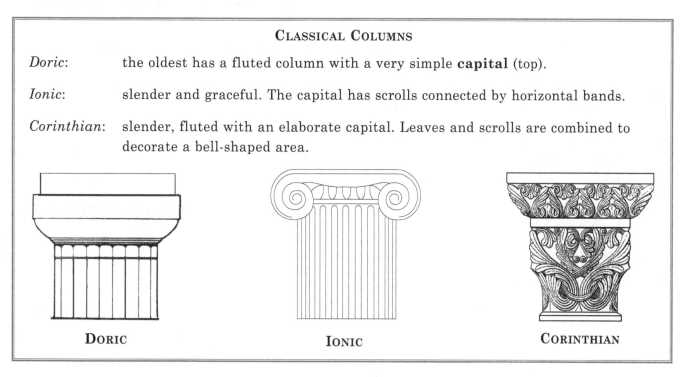

CLASSICAL COLUMNS

Doric: the oldest has a fluted column with a very simple **capital** (top).

Ionic: slender and graceful. The capital has scrolls connected by horizontal bands.

Corinthian: slender, fluted with an elaborate capital. Leaves and scrolls are combined to decorate a bell-shaped area.

DORIC   **IONIC**   **CORINTHIAN**

From approximately 1100–1400, Gothic architecture reached its peak in the design of churches and glowing stained glass windows.

This style is distinguished by the use of ribbed vaults, pointed arches and jewel-like stained glass. It produces an inspirational atmosphere by emphasizing a sweeping design focused upward, toward God.

Paris' Notre Dame Cathedral is one of its most famous examples. Begun in A.D. 1163, its construction (a community effort) took approximately 90 years. It was the first to use flying buttresses.

NOTRE DAME CATHEDRAL, PARIS, FRANCE

Photo: Ed Shea

LLOYD WRIGHT'S WAYFARER'S CHAPEL

Wayfarer's Chapel of The Church of the New Jerusalem in Rancho Palos Verdes, California, was designed by contemporary American architect Lloyd Wright, son of Frank Lloyd Wright (a leader of the modern architectural revolution). Wayfarer's Chapel is modern, airy, and light; a marked contrast to the stone towers of Notre Dame.

Rather than focusing the attention upward to God, the focus is on Creation and ourselves, the glass walls clearly showing nearby scenic beauty. Its intent was to focus on the "harmony" between nature and our "inner" spiritual world.

Exercise 3.3

Answer this question.

3.16   Why is architecture unique as a fine art?

_____

_____

Match the architectural style with its description.

3.17   _____   Colonial

3.18   _____   Prairie

3.19   _____   Victorian

3.20   _____   Organic

3.21   _____   Amalgamated

a. one of the earliest in America (as indicated in its name)

b. a renaissance of Greek and Roman forms

c. borrows from the Gothic revival and has ornate wood detailing

3.22 _____ Classical Revival

3.23 _____ International

3.24 _____ Bungalow

d. low, flat appearance and horizontal design

e. originated with the English in India, Bengali house

f. concerned with environmental concerns of light and air

g. imaginary, an attempt to better fit nature

h. attempt to combine too many materials and styles

Name and describe the three classical columns.

3.25

3.26

3.27

3.25 _____

_____

3.26 _____

_____

3.27 _____

_____

Give the best answer.

3.28 For what purpose were Greek temples built?

_____

_____

3.29 What was the intended result of Gothic architecture's inspirational atmosphere?

_____

_____

3.30   What was the intent of the glass-encased, airy and light design of Wayfarer's Chapel?

_____

_____

APPLIED AND COMMERCIAL ART

Art created for a practical use is called **applied art**, which includes architecture, tableware, wall hangings, tapestries and furniture.

Photography. A photographer's medium is film. Through design, exposure, lighting and chemical techniques, photographers create art, capturing the same emotions that great paintings can.

For example, in *Looking for a Friend*, the photographer caught the dog in a pose of seeming loneliness. The large amount of background makes the dog look smaller and more alone.

Courtesy of Giant Photos, Rockford, Il.

LOOKING FOR A FRIEND

Ansel Adams (1902–1984), is possibly America's best-known photographer. He created beautiful landscapes with impeccable exposure and printing. During the Great Depression, he was commissioned by the Federal Government to photograph national landmarks, such as Hoover Dam and Glacier National Park. His photographs can be used as an excellent record of recent U.S. history.

National Archives

ANSEL ADAMS' EVENING, MCDONALD LAKE, GLACIER NATIONAL PARK, MONTANA

Commercial Art. Art created for publications are the dominant outlets for artistic talent today. Illustrations, advertisements and cartoons are all **commercial art**, typically sold by themselves or in order to sell a product. Although used exclusively to make money, the aesthetic value of commercial art must not be dismissed. It is by far the most popular and easily accessible form of artistic expression in the modern world.

Since 1900, when commercial art got its start, its importance has skyrocketed. Originally, all commercial artists were self–taught, but today several schools and universities offer degrees in the subject.

PRINT ADS ARE AN EXAMPLE OF COMMERCIAL ART.

CARTOONS ARE ANOTHER EXAMPLE OF COMMERCIAL ART.

 Exercise 3.4 Answer these questions

3.31 Define applied art.

_____

3.32 What is the photographer's medium?

_____

3.33 Who commissioned Ansel Adams' photographs? During what era?

_____

3.34 What is the exclusive purpose of commercial art?

_____

3.35 Why shouldn't the aesthetic value of commercial art be dismissed?

_____

Before you take this last Self Test, you may want to do one or more of these self checks.

1. _____ Read the objectives. Determine if you can do them.

2. _____ Restudy the material related to any objectives that you cannot do.

3. _____ Use the SQ3R study procedure to review the material:
   a. **S**can the sections.
   b. **Q**uestion yourself again (review the questions you wrote initially).
   c. **R**ead to answer your questions.
   d. **R**ecite the answers to yourself.
   e. **R**eview areas you didn't understand.

4. _____ Review all vocabulary, activities, and Self Tests, writing a correct answer for each wrong answer.

SELF TEST 3

Answer the questions (each question 10 points).

3.01 What is the most popular painted subject in history? Why?

_____

3.02 When was the great period of mural painting?

_____

3.03 Define sculpture.

_____

3.04 Define relief as it pertains to sculpture.

_____

3.05 Why is architecture unique as a fine art?

_____

3.06 For what purpose were Greek temples built?

_____

3.07 What was the intended result of Gothic architecture's inspirational atmosphere?

_____

3.08 Define applied art.

_____

3.09 What was the exclusive purpose of commercial art?

_____

3.10 Why shouldn't the aesthetic value of commercial art be dismissed?

_____

80 /
/ 100

Score _____

Instructor Check _____

Initial   Date

EVALUATION

Now that you have completed *Art Appreciation*, glance back at your original expectations. Did you learn what you expected? How was the Unit different than your expectations?

_____

_____

_____

_____

_____

_____

_____

Explain three new things you learned while studying this Unit, as if explaining it to someone unfamiliar with the subject.

What is the most important thing you learned in this Unit?

_____

_____

_____

_____

_____

_____

_____

_____

_____

_____

_____

_____

_____

_____

_____

_____

GLOSSARY

Aesthetics—The study of beauty and art.

Aesthetic experience—The fusion of pleasure and learning as a work of art is viewed.

Applied art—Art created for practical uses.

Capital—Top of a column.

Concept—The philosophical content of a work of art, the moral or message.

Commercial art—Art created for publications.

Criticism—Evaluating a work to determine its value.

Elements of art—Line, shape, texture, color and value.

Elements of design—Balance, proportion, rhythm, dominance and unity.

Form—The beauty of design and order in order to communicate clearly.

Freestanding—Sculpture that is surrounded on all sides by space.

Intaglio—A relief in reverse; the image is cut into a surface rather than raised from a background.

In the Round—A freestanding sculpture that can be viewed from all sides.

Landscape—Picture of natural, inland scenery such as mountains, prairies, woodlands, etc.

Relief—Sculpture is raised against a background.

Seascape—Picture of a view of the ocean, often containing at least a portion of the beach.

Sculpture—Three dimensional art carved out of or molded from a substance.

 Before you take the Unit Test, you may want to do one or more of these self checks.

1. _____ Read the objectives. Determine if you can do them.

2. _____ Restudy the material related to any objectives that you cannot do.

3. _____ Use the SQ3R study procedure to review the material.

4. _____ Review all activities and Self Tests, and Unit Glossary.

5. _____ Restudy areas of weakness indicated by the last Self Test.